When the wind
blows through you like a
SCREAM

Written and illustrated by
Carolkay MacKay

Cover photo by Brett Wilkins
Photo, pg. 42, by W.R. McGowan
Published by Carolkay Designs, © 2000

Printed by Ojai Printing and Publishing Co.
111 N. Blanche Street
Ojai, CA   93023

Stay clear of the
    long dark shadows
let them keep their
            secrets

Windows

she woke to the sound of
engines banging at the air
- shuddering into her sleep -
shouldering into her neck of quiet

she bolted like some piece of
thrown cloth unraveling in the wind -
metal sounds ripping her apart
          exposing the cold wet eye
               whistling away

the fence of reality alarmingly
close, rippling across the surface of
her silence like thrown stones;
skipping at the beat of her heart,
she reached out into the neck of
the dark and slipped away

where in the shift of presence
did she belong? not here, certainly,
among the metallic ring of stones
heaved into walls that bind; not in
the rope of thought that twists the
soul and anchors away the mind

humanity pressed against her,
all hands about her throat; she
clawed free of its weight

suspended in the liquid void just
long enough to feel

across the wind the boundless reach
of faith come flying

to lift the soul and tear no more
                              and heal

3

this book starts with a scream;
by its end i learned
the longer we scream
the more we miss

this book is like the wall in my studio:
papered with drawings, poems,
cartoons, notes to myself,

and a photograph of a man in a wheelchair
using a computer by means of a long
wooden stick held between his teeth

he, with all the more reason to scream,
misses little

when i feel a scream coming on,
i think about that young man's
courage and strength and determination

and i cram a stick into my hand
and get on with it

life is about Focus

to focus mostly on yourself

is to never get out the

front door

there was a woman
whose neighborhood was becoming
increasingly violent - one afternoon
she lay down and tried to sleep with
all the violence outside -
she dreamed she lived life the best
she could -
she was a positive influence
and in a small way lessened
the violence -
her positive energy spread
through-out the community, until
everyone was striving to be their
best scenario -
when everyone became their
own best dream, suddenly she was
surrounded by violence -
she never dreamed that anyone's
best dreams could be anything
but good -
she never considered that
anyone's best dreams could
be negative

then she woke up - to the sound of

VIOLENCE

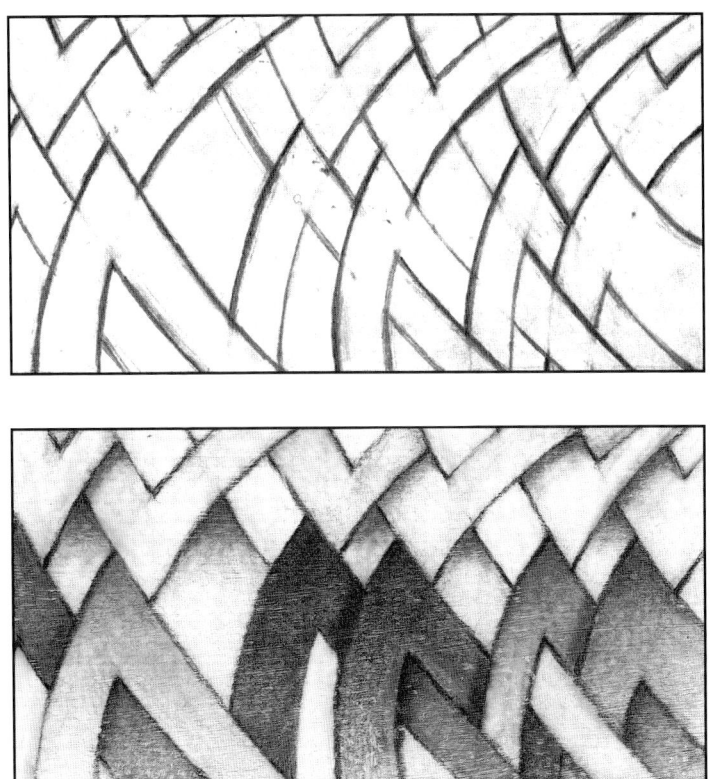

                        she

                                pushed her hands
down her legs in the warm water -
pushed ahead of her all the
negatives: work, pressure, time,
all that seized

                                pushed them out of her body
- a flood of peace rushing in
to fill the naked space,
trailing her hands like sun
come into the hollows

her skin like silk in
the water - the air bodied with the
sweetness of camomile - the water a
thick elixir of the herb

slipped her hands down her legs -
stripped off the old skin in sheets
that wandered off like wands of silk

new skin soft as old satin
air the scent of honey
a new moment
in her hands

Parallax

i sink into a
tub of hot water
the water in me responds to
the water around me

i am no longer a body in a
tub -
    but a shell

the waters rise within me
as though i am an idea
through which they travel

i settle deeper into the tub
and feel the rhythm in the water

i slow my breathing, conscious
now of the waves -
   my breath slows until
it comes into harmony with
the waves

suddenly we are one,
the water
& i

            the water is an idea
              through which
                i travel

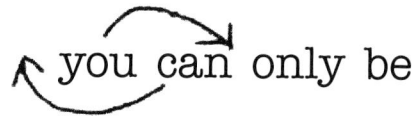 you can only be

less

than what you think

you

are

when i was a kid
i went from imagining
myself as invisible -
to being invisible but
also able to fly -
to leaving my body
  as a sure way of
    escape

when an atom changes into

pure energy ~

does it retain its memory?

is memory pure energy

in material form?

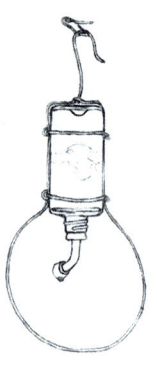

what about
thought?

what's the conversion
of mass to
energy

there?

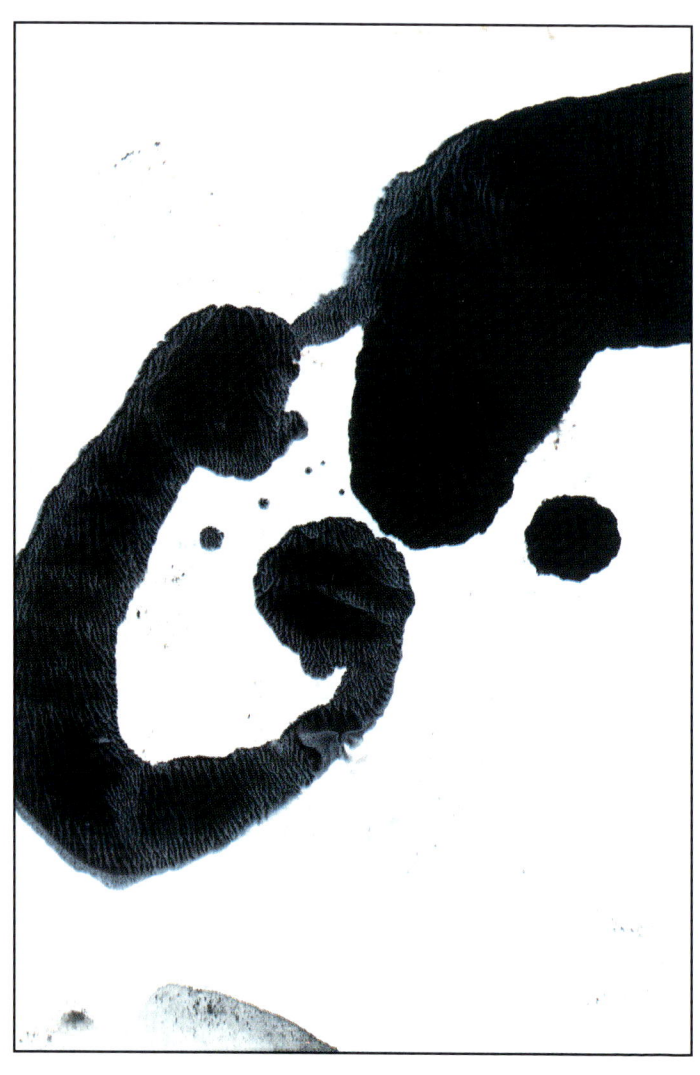

life is an
emanation
that meets itself
somewhere

we sit on the couch
my left side to your right side
& we lie in bed your left side to
my right side -

what if we always related from
my
left to your right? would we
come
to know only half of each
other?

do we cross-relate
when we face each other?
or
do our minds meet directly
straight across?

if you're left-handed &
i'm right-handed, does the
energy from your
right-brain to your left hand
go from your left hand to my
right-brain & so on..........?

i like the irony in thinking about

a woman who wrote into Reality, &
found herself one day writing not
what she was thinking but something
else
as she read what she had written,
she realised she had tapped into
memories that stretched infinitely
in all directions

there were a few at first, but then
they crowded in & filled
every space until she could
no longer discern which was Herself,
if indeed she was there
at all

it's ok to be the
person you want to be

it's better to be the
person that you are

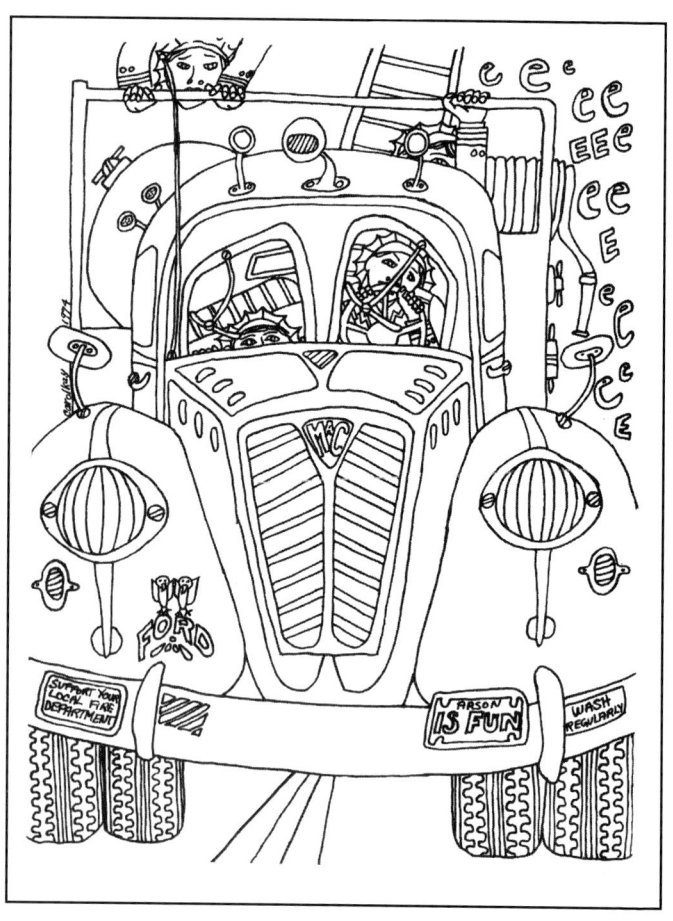

there's a general
consensus of dogs in the
neighborhood that something's
not quite right

i try to imagine what it
might be like to have
conversation with others
that you've never seen -
to get to know someone only
through the sounds
they're able to make

~~living~~
life is learning
how to breathe
through someone
else's skin

C. ANDREWS

life can be very
shallow-

living has depth

if you spend all your time
thinking about yesterday

then all your memories
will be
reruns

yesterday was the end of
an
ERA

Today -   is a whole new

CONCEPT

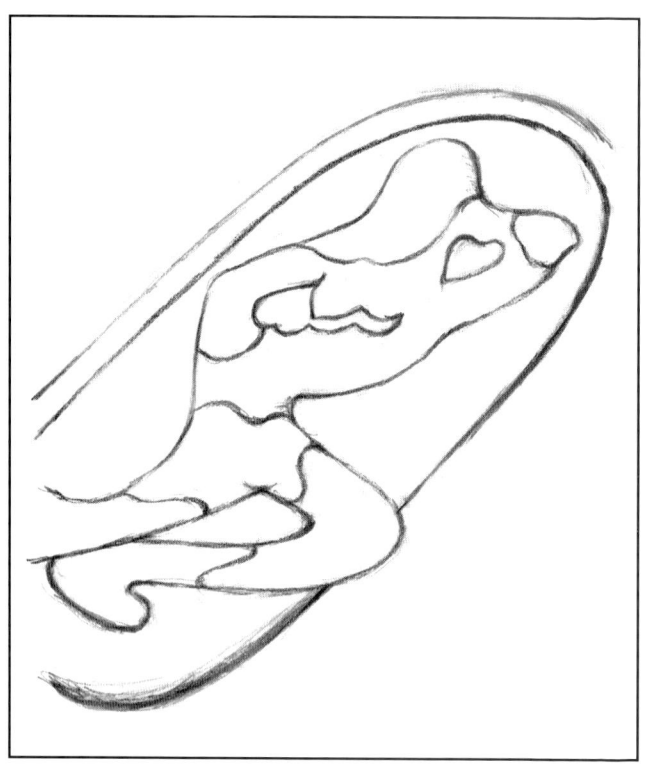

do you ever lie in the tub as the
water's draining out & visualize
yourself as a Henry Moore sculpture
with part of you sticking out above the
water
sticking out more in places
you'd rather you didn't & not
sticking out enough in others

you feel yourself into the shape
& you move with the body of the
sculpture

like taking a roller coaster ride through
the giant form &
suddenly you're inside the wood
and come to know

                              the tree

carol kay 1993

if you don't get
your
face into life

your existence
goes Unnoticed

there are no paths
with gilded sunshine edges
macrame of rose & orange & spice

somewhere we've been misled &
try to walk a non-existent road

with lives somewhat peripheral
we pass now & then over a core

glimpsing its essence, we pass on

we try to stay in bounds
to make a path of certainty
we try to Be the core

somewhere here there is a
lesson in
free
flight

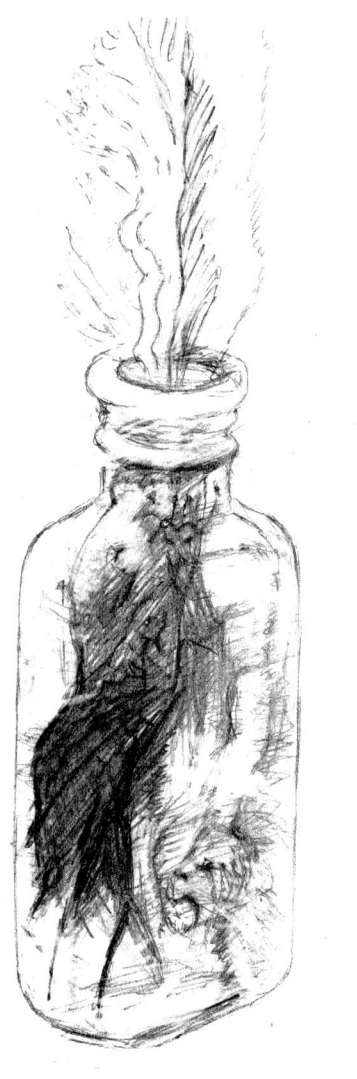

40

i'm looking at a glass bottle which
culminates in three feathers-
i close my right eye & notice a
change in shadows-   i look with my
right eye only & everything is so
much smaller ~   so much more
detailed

i never noticed this difference
before
i look through different eyes to
discover exactly what the difference
is-   it's more than closer & farther-
more than light & dark-   more than
left-brain & right-brain

it's a space-time difference
like seeing in two places & time-zones
at the same time
with the bottle

somewhere in the middle

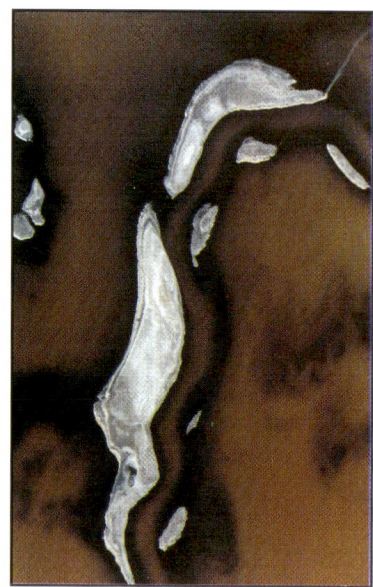

Photo by W.R. McGowan

                    it's not
what the eye can see that i'm
trying to get at-   it's the
        spaces in between

we're a continually changing mass
    driven by electrical impulses-

    we're walking conversions
  of matter to energy and back
  again- and we're also those
                instants
  when one becomes the other
          the invisible instant
      the other possibilities

            the spACES
    in   between

we do not die into
                    nothing

we die into something;

we are not born of nothing

*rather exalt
than be
exalted*

Faith is Divine Trust

It is God-Given

Would that He Receive

As Much As

He Gives

measure yourself by
the love
that you give

rather than
by the love
that you
receive

if you don't get your
Face into life

your EXISTENCE
goes
UNnoticed

your Face was put here
for a
Reason!

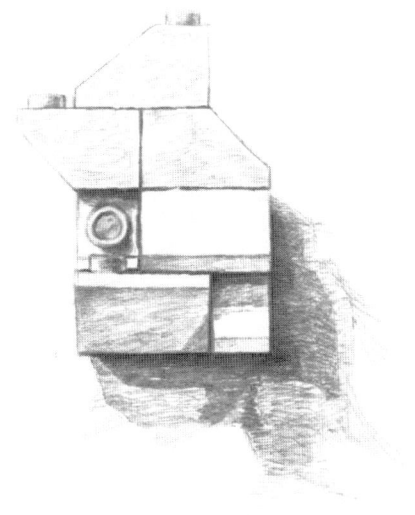

to approach life

with a

FIXED IDEA

is to limit

its

possibilities

imagination
is the creation of images from
experiences conjoined at
varying levels
from molecular
to quantum

?

OUT

get

you

do

how

&

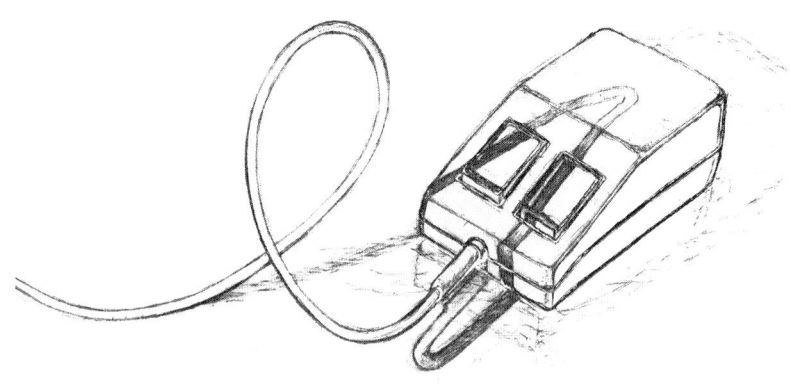

What will the world be like when

we have Full Screen TV? NOT the kind

that wraps around the walls, but

where you're in the center of a TV

screen - it projects all around you

& you float weightless in the center

immersed in sounds & images

maybe you have a joystick that

changes the action - you feel like

you're in control, but you're still

always in someone Else's dream

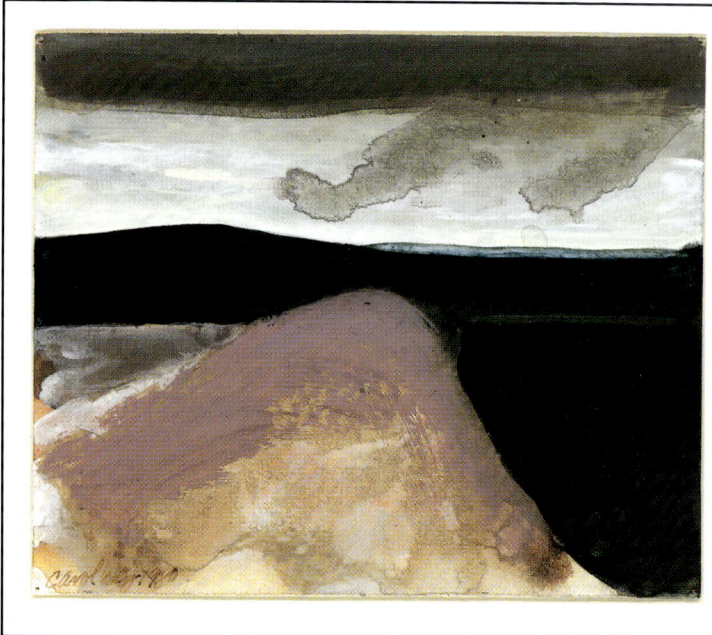

it is not enough to
be a reflection

when we are called
it is with our own
    light
that we answer

Pearl Harbor Day

we've gone so far FORWARD to be so
FAR BACK

i don't understand ---
i thought PEACE was making headway
i thought DECENCY had a chance

i thought we knew our
EXISTENCE was in the
BALANCE

but we never learned to
DANCE - we watched, & then we
TURNED AWAY

and the soldiers once were weavers
whom the rich men sent to death

light passing through a point is
forever altered

as life passing through a person is
forever altered

& how does your silhouette stand
in the quiet of the dark?

what are you against the sky?

be careful what you

ARE

what you are reaches

touches

Forever

Charles (Bob) and
Norma Andrews

This book
is dedicated
to my parents
whose love,
enthusiasm for life
&
deep reverence
for Spirit
echo
through these
pages